MAY THE ROAD
RISE TO MEET YOU

MAY THE ROAD RISE TO MEET YOU

A 31-DAY DEVOTIONAL
INSPIRED BY IRISH BLESSINGS

Jennifer Deibel

Revell

a division of Baker Publishing Group
Grand Rapids, Michigan

© 2026 by Jennifer Deibel

Published by Revell
a division of Baker Publishing Group
Grand Rapids, Michigan
RevellBooks.com

Printed in China

Library of Congress Cataloging-in-Publication Data
Names: Deibel, Jennifer, 1978– author.
Title: May the road rise to meet you : a 31-day devotional inspired by Irish blessings / Jennifer Deibel.
Description: Grand Rapids, Michigan : Revell, a division of Baker Publishing Group, [2026]
Identifiers: LCCN 2025008488 | ISBN 9780800745998 (cloth) | ISBN 9781493452682 (ebook)
Subjects: LCSH: Devotional calendars. | Prayer.
Classification: LCC BV4811 .D425 2026 | DDC 242/.2—dc23/eng/20250815
LC record available at https://lccn.loc.gov/2025008488

Cover design by Laura Klynstra

Published in association with Books & Such Literary Management, www.booksandsuch.com.

Baker Publishing Group publications use paper produced from sustainable forestry practices and postconsumer waste whenever possible.

26 27 28 29 30 31 32   7 6 5 4 3 2 1

BEFORE YOU BEGIN

Céad Míle Fáilte, **Dear Friend!**

You are most welcome! I am so honored and delighted that you've chosen to join me for these thirty-one days as we explore and enjoy some of the world's most beloved blessings, revel in the magical and inviting Irish culture, and soak in God's Word.

It is my prayer that after this month, you will experience a deeper faith and a closer walk with God and that you'll carry a more profound appreciation for the beauty and depth of the Irish art of a blessing.

I lived in Ireland with my family for just over six years, and it completely changed my life and worldview. Along with being the Land of Forty Shades of Green, Ireland is also known as the Land of Blessings and Curses. Even the most basic phrases—like hello and goodbye—are actually blessings! The traditional greeting of *Dia dhuit* literally means "God to you," and when you part ways and call s*lán* over your shoulder, you're offering a prayer for health and safety! God permeates almost everything about the Irish culture—whether the average person realizes or even fully believes in Him. The culture of speaking in blessings is rooted in the core belief that words have the power to bring life . . . or death. Funny, since the Bible says exactly that!

> The tongue has the power of life and death,
>   and those who love it will eat its fruit.
>   (Prov. 18:21 NIV)

This way of looking at the world and speaking to one another has had such an impact on the way I think, speak, and act, and I wanted to share it with you as well. Each entry will include an Irish blessing, a few Scripture references that relate to the theme, a devotional thought from my heart, and a suggestion for how to pray and apply the day's reading.

Of course, dear friend, as wonderful and uplifting as these blessings are, God's Word is even more so! In Isaiah 55:11, God promises us that His Word will not return void, and it is through His Word and the Holy Spirit that our hearts are truly changed. Because of this, I invite you to join me in another Irish tradition—slowing down to put relationships first. Sit with me and the Father and let your heart really connect with His. I promise you won't walk away from these thirty-one days unchanged, and you'll probably be breathing a little easier by the end too.

If you don't own a Bible and are unable to purchase one, you can find free options online. A personal favorite of mine is BibleGateway.com. There's also a free Bible app you can download onto your electronic device.

While sitting down for a cuppa with a close Irish friend often spans several hours, this devotional is designed to be completed in about fifteen minutes. But you are, of course, welcome to spend as much time as your heart needs. You'll find space at the end of each entry to journal your thoughts or write out your prayers. By the end of our time together, my hope is that this book will feel like a cozy blanket or your favorite pair of slippers, bringing comfort and joy to your soul.

Let's enjoy this time together. Savor the blessings, the Scriptures, and your conversations with God. When you're done, I'd love to hear how your faith grew or your relationship with God deepened along the way! Drop me a note at Jennifer@JenniferDeibel.com.

Blessings,
Jen

DAY
1

May the road rise up to meet you.

May the wind be always at your back.

May the sun shine warm upon your face;

the rains fall soft upon your fields and until we meet again,

may God hold you in the palm of His hand.

TRADITIONAL IRISH BLESSING

TODAY'S READING: Matthew 11:28–30; John 16:33

"May the road rise up to meet you" is arguably the most well-known Irish blessing/prayer in the world. Often recited during times of change or major life transition—like marriage, a new job, or moving away—this word gift speaks of ease in life, the benefit of creature comforts, and reconnecting with loved ones when time and/or distance separate them.

Some schools of thought propose that this ancient blessing has deeper theological roots, with the wind representing the Holy Spirit, the sun referring to God's mercy (as spoken of in Zechariah's prophecy in Luke 1), and the rain symbolizing God's provision.*

It warmed my heart to find that theory in my research. So often we think of God's blessing as relieving strain or stress to make our lives as comfortable as possible. At first

---

*James Wilson, "'May the Road Rise Up to Meet You'—The Story Behind the Traditional Irish Blessing," Irish Central, September 19, 2023, https://www.irishcentral.com/culture/may-the-road-rise-meet-you-irish -blessing-meaning.

glance, that's what that famous Irish prayer is asking for on behalf of a loved one.

But if we examine God's Word closely, as in the Scriptures you read today, we see that God's true blessing is the indwelling of His Holy Spirit, His presence and guidance in our daily lives, and His provision in His perfect timing.

John 16:33 promises us that we will have troubles in life, and Matthew 11:28–30 guides us to acknowledge that God is with us even when we are tired, weary, and burdened.

Oddly, one of my favorite Irish endearments is one that's commonly shared at funerals. When greeting the mourning family, one might offer a phrase of condolence that literally translates to "I don't like your troubles." This utterance does not make the trouble of grief disappear but rather promises presence *through* the troubles. This causes me to ask the question, *What do we do when those hard times come*? Do we beg God to take them away and bring us a little slice of paradise? Or do we look for where He is in the difficult circumstances so we can join Him, follow Him, and see where He wants to work both in and through us?

APPLY IT: Are you looking for the easy way out? Is there some aspect of your life in which you're trying to avoid the challenging road? Pray and ask God to show Himself to you within that circumstance. He will walk through it with you.

DAY
2

May brooks and trees and singing hills

Join in the chorus too

And every gentle wind that blows

Send happiness to you.

— TRADITIONAL IRISH BLESSING —

TODAY'S READING: Psalm 19; Luke 19:28–40

I have never been accused of being an "outdoorsy girl." I've grown up in big cities my whole life, and most of my formative years were spent in that context. While I don't hate the outdoors, it is not my preferred setting.

However, some of the most moving and endearing moments I've spent with the Lord have been amid His creation.

When we lived in Ireland, I took up running. There was just something about being in that fresh salty air, running along the coastline with the turquoise Atlantic on one side and an emerald patchwork of fields on the other that stirred my soul. As though creation itself beckoned me to come and see God's goodness.

As children of the 80s and 90s, we witnessed a pendulum swing away from nature as a way to experience God. This was due mainly to the sudden rise in New Age beliefs and ideologies that worshiped not the Creator but what had been created. And as we are often wont to do, we may have thrown the baby out with the bathwater.

The psalmist pairs nature with God's teaching toward the end of Psalm 19. He begins by admiring and declaring the beauty of God's creation, describing the many incredible ways God shows Himself through the nature He crafted. Then it's as if all the evidence stretched before him in the form of an azure sky dotted with cotton clouds and brilliant sunshine, and his eyes are opened for the first time. At this point he transitions from admiring creation itself to recognizing how it reflects its Maker, then understanding how that creation expresses the goodness and righteousness of the Lord.

> The instruction of the LORD is perfect . . .
> the testimony of the LORD is trustworthy . . .
> The precepts of the LORD are right . . .
> the command of the LORD is radiant . . .
> The fear of the LORD is pure . . .
> the ordinances of the LORD are reliable
> and altogether righteous. (Ps. 19:7–9 CSB)

Then the psalmist weaves in how those things affect us, God's children: They're life renewing (v. 7); they make the heart glad and the eyes light up (v. 8). Last, His attributes last forever. So if you are struggling to connect with God, get out in His creation—even if it's just for a couple of minutes.

APPLY IT: Get out in creation today: Take a walk around the block, sit outside on your lunch break, or get out for a hike if the weather permits. Meditate on today's verses and offer your own thanks and admiration back to God as you do.

DAY
3

May the grace of God's protection

And His great love abide

Within your home,

Within the hearts

Of all who dwell inside.

TRADITIONAL IRISH BLESSING

TODAY'S READING: Deuteronomy 6:1–9; Psalm 133; 2 Corinthians 13:5–13

There's just something special about home, isn't there? One of my favorite Irish phrases is "*Níl aon tinteán mar do thinteán féin*," which translates to "There's no hearth like your own hearth." But as beautiful a sentiment as that is, the truth is that home is a unique and complicated place—one that can often change depending on your life circumstances.

No matter if you're a teen still living at home, a college student sharing a dorm or apartment, a newlywed couple, a parent, an empty nester, or a widow/widower living alone again, God has a lot to say about what goes on at home.

Today's Irish blessing so beautifully echoes the message of Scripture—specifically the passages listed for today's reading. Though, truth be told, I could have listed tons more that relate to the peace of Christ abiding in our home.

No matter what blend of people currently live at home with you, you cannot control anyone but yourself. As a mom, I long for my children to choose to love and follow Jesus and to daily grow in their relationship with Him. I can pray to that end, but whether they do or not is entirely out of my control.

Often we lift up prayers asking God to work change in the hearts of those in our homes—and there is nothing wrong with that—but we would be wise to pay attention when Paul says, "Test yourselves to see if you are in the faith. Examine yourselves" (2 Cor. 13:5 CSB).

This examination is not to form a distorted, self-centered pseudo-faith but rather to see the plank in our own eyes before we attempt to get the speck out of the eyes of those we live with (see Matt. 7:3–5).

Instead, we should focus on deepening our own faith and cultivating a heart of Christ's love through our relationship with Him. Then we can allow the changes He makes in us to inspire that same heart of grace—and God's protection against bitterness, anger, and brokenness—to sink roots deep into our homes.

APPLY IT: How is the atmosphere within your home? Is it full of grace and peace? Or does it feel tense and heavy? Do those who live there treat one another with kindness and respect? Or is it everyone for themselves? Spend a few moments meditating on today's Scriptures, then ask God to cover your home with His grace. Ask Him what one thing you need to do or say today for His love to more fully abide within your home.

DAY
4

May peace and plenty bless your world

With a joy that long endures.

And may all life's passing seasons

Bring the best to you and yours.

TRADITIONAL IRISH BLESSING

TODAY'S READING: John 15:9–12; Romans 5:1–5; Philippians 4:4–9; (bonus: 1 John 1)

In Ireland—particularly in the coastal areas where we lived—gale force winds are a near daily experience in the winter. And all the rest of the year. It isn't uncommon for the winds to stir up regularly.

I used to peer out onto the bay from our living room windows and see how many whitecaps were dancing on the water's surface. It always made me grateful when it was unseasonably calm. Of course, everyone was elated when the wind died down, the sun came out, and the world seemed at peace. Or at least that small, emerald corner of it, anyway.

But inevitably someone would point out that the peace was never going to last. You could almost set your watch by it. "Ah, well, 'tis grand now, but just ye wait. It'll change," they'd say. And we'd all murmur and nod, because we knew it to be true.

I find myself doing the same thing in my own life even now. I long for the peaceful quiet of the absence of conflict, but when it comes, I know it won't last. That's why I'm so grateful for both today's blessing and the accompanying Scriptures. Because God's Word tells us exactly how to find that lasting peace that defies logic. We can simply:

- present everything to Him in prayer, with thanks-giving (see Phil. 4:6)
- put our faith in Jesus and allow Him, through our faith, to declare us righteous (see Rom. 5:1)
- recognize and embrace that our struggles and dif-ficulties refine our character, if we remain in Him (see Rom. 5:3–5)
- remain in Him—stay, linger, soak in His presence—and let His love flow through us (see John 15:9–10)

This peace reaches beyond the direst of circumstances and settles deep in the core of our souls. It remains when life is chaotic and we feel like a leaf blown on a gale. It enriches our joy as we celebrate milestones and victories. And it guides us when the fog of uncertainty settles over our hearts.

If you are not sure how to put your faith in Him, con-sider the bonus Scripture for today. In it, John very clearly lays out that we need to admit to God that we've missed the mark. When we do, Jesus will cleanse us, forgive us, and make us right in the eyes of our Father (1 John 1:9).

APPLY IT: Does peace seem fleeting to you, like it's floating just out of reach? Choose one of today's passages and pray it back to God, asking Him to solidify His peace in your heart.

DAY
5

If God sends you down a stony path

May He give you strong shoes.

TRADITIONAL IRISH BLESSING

TODAY'S READING: Isaiah 40:28–31; Matthew 7:13–14; Hebrews 13:20–21

Have you ever stepped on a LEGO barefoot? Or perhaps a grass burr? Few things bring me to tears more quickly than those two events. So when I learned that some people climb a mountain in Ireland barefoot, I had to know more— mainly so I could understand it but also so I could understand how best to avoid it.

On the last Sunday in July, thousands upon thousands of pilgrims climb Croagh Patrick in County Mayo. It is here that Saint Patrick is believed to have fasted for forty days and nights before driving all the snakes out of Ireland. So on a set day designated to honor his actions, people climb. And those who climb barefoot do so as an act of penance to pay for their sins and shortcomings. It's a three-hour round trip on a rocky path that leads to a peak made of quartzite, and they choose to do it without shoes.

Jesus never once promises us that following Him will be easy, always fun, or completely problem-free. In fact, as we saw in day 1, He promises us the exact opposite. But He does promise to be with us every step of the way (Heb. 13:5). And, as we read in today's verses, He also promises to equip us for wherever He leads us and for whatever task or situation He leads us to.

In Matthew 7, He tells us clearly that following the crowd leads to death. That road is wide, he says, and plenty of people will make their way down it. But the better way, the true way—*His* way—is narrow.

When we look around and see very few people following the path we're on, it can be tempting to assume we've made a wrong turn. We look at the obstacles in our way and begin to doubt. We glance at the trail across the valley, see the multitudes making their way along it, and think that's where we need to be. But Jesus reminds us His ways are upside down to the world.

We do not need to take our spiritual fate into our own hands by choosing to walk that wide, stony path on our bare skin to convince Him to forgive us. He's already paid the price for us, endured that unimaginable pain, and carried the emotional, spiritual, and eternal consequences of our sins. And because of that, we are free to accept the proverbial strong shoes today's Irish blessing speaks of.

Yes, following and obeying the Lord can be challenging. It will lead us down some stony paths. But He has given us all we need to navigate them in a way that shows His power and grace to others.

APPLY IT: Are you on a tough path right now? Does it feel like you're walking barefoot on LEGOs? Ask God to help you accept His strength and let Him equip you for all He's called you to.

DAY
6

May the raindrops fall lightly on your brow.

May the soft winds freshen your spirit.

May the sunshine brighten your heart.

May the burdens of the day rest lightly upon you.

And may God enfold you in His love.

TRADITIONAL IRISH BLESSING

TODAY'S READING: Matthew 11:25–30; 1 Peter 5:6–7, 10

I grew up in the Arizona desert. That's where I spent the majority of my formative years. We were accustomed to being able to go outside just about any time of year to have a picnic, play baseball, go for a walk, visit a fair or festival, or whatever we fancied. And when it rained, everything shut down. To be honest, it was kind of nice when it rained. Unless, of course, we were really looking forward to the event that had to be canceled.

When we moved to Ireland, we went from one of the least rained-on places in the world to a land that has one of the highest numbers of rainy days. To say it was a shock to the system would be an understatement.

It didn't take us long, however, to realize that the Irish way of life meant that if we canceled something because it was raining . . . well, we'd never do anything! And that's exactly what came to mind when I read today's Irish blessing.

If we wait to spend time with God, pray, or share our faith until we are burden or problem free, we will never get around to it. Today's blessing references the rain, wind, and troubles and prays that they would be lighter and that we would be able to handle them with ease through the filter of God's love. And there's the secret.

I love the reminder that we get in today's verses to bring our burdens to Jesus—the One Who not only knows and understands our burdens but also knows why we endure them. Not only that but He promises that when we come to Him and give over our worries and heavy hearts, He carries them and replaces them with His burden, which is light and easy (see Matt. 11:30).

So, when you're sinking under the weight of all you're carrying, come to Jesus. Lay your burdens in His hands and rest in Him. The Bible also says that none of these troubles will last forever, and when they are over, He will restore, establish, strengthen, and support you. And that, dear friend, is the greatest blessing.

APPLY IT: What burdens are you carrying today? Reread today's Scripture passages and turn those promises back to Him in prayer. Then share with someone what you are asking Him to carry and let that person walk with you.

DAY
7

May you always have walls for the winds,
A roof for the rain, tea beside the fire,
Laughter to cheer you, those you love near you,
And all your heart might desire.

TRADITIONAL IRISH BLESSING

TODAY'S READING: Matthew 6:25–34; Philippians 4:19; Hebrews 13:5

Winter in Ireland can be a wild time. My family and I used to hunker down in our sitting room, warmed by the roaring turf fire, and watch as the windows flexed and our car rocked violently in the driveway amid the intense weather raging outside. But perhaps where the weather seemed fiercest was upstairs.

Irish homes often feature windows in their slanted rooves. While the extra light they afford is wonderful, on a stormy night they also create the loudest ruckus you've ever heard. And every night, like clockwork, once the racket started, I had approximately thirty seconds before two tiny girls were in our bed, crying in fear at the terrible noise. It was on those same nights I would lie there, bleary-eyed, wishing for "normal" windows that allowed me the sleep I so desperately longed for.

But deep down I was so very grateful for the safety and shelter of the sturdy house where we could weather the daily torrents of those long, dark winter months.

We weren't always sure we would have a safe place to call home in Ireland. When it came time to find a house, the options that fit within our budget were slim to none. Many nights my husband and I huddled together in the vacation home we had rented while we looked, wondering why God would lead us to this country if He wasn't going to provide a place for us to live.

And as our family has grown and our children have gotten older and begun to leave the nest, those prayers of desperation have never really gone away. And I suspect it's the same for you.

Scripture commands that we should not worry about what we eat, drink, wear, or where we live, because God promises to provide (Matt. 6:25–33). But there are times when our circumstances seem to stand in direct contrast to that. There were times when we didn't know where our next meal would come from or how we would pay the mortgage that month, and then He miraculously provided. And yet I've met people living on the streets who love Jesus just as much as I do.

I don't have an answer as to why God allows dire situations for some of us and not for others. But I've learned that God's definitions and mine can be very different, and that's okay. Our job is to trust and obey when He says to move or act.

APPLY IT: Where are you struggling to trust God's provision today? Choose one of today's verses, meditate on it, and pray it back to God through the lens of that circumstance. Then thank Him in advance for answering your prayer, asking Him to open your eyes wide to see when He does.

DAY
8

May the friendships you make,

Be those which endure,

And all of your grey clouds

Be small ones for sure.

And trusting in Him

To Whom we all pray,

May a song fill your heart,

Every step of the way.

TRADITIONAL IRISH BLESSING

TODAY'S READING: Proverbs 18:24; Ecclesiastes 4:9–12; Romans 12:9–19

There's a place in Galway where the city streets meet the bay and the red sails of the Hooker boats glide across the water in peace. Just about any time of day, people walk along a path nearby called The Long Walk.

Less than a quarter of a mile long, The Long Walk really isn't that long, but it is always teeming with people. It was stormy out the first time I walked it. Rain pelted me and my friends, and waves splashed over the retaining wall onto the path. Had I not been with Aisling and Debra, I most certainly would not have been out there that night.

But we'd committed to walking together several days a week. You see, there's a reason Ireland is known as the Land of Forty Shades of Green. Its west coast can see upwards of 118 inches of rain a year! So, I embraced my newfound Irishness and ventured out into the storm with my friends.

On these walks, it was sometimes hard to muster up the motivation to get out there and do what I said I would do when the winds and storms of the world swirled around us. That's where Aisling, Debra, and several others came in.

These dear women took me by the proverbial hand and helped me keep my promises to myself and those around me—even when the world seemed to be crashing down all around. I'm happy to say I was able to do the same for them.

That's how it works in our faith journey as well. We need like-minded people to walk alongside and bolster us when the storms of life threaten to drown us. We were created for community, and even the most introverted person was designed to do life with others.

It can be tempting to withdraw into ourselves, especially during seasons of struggle. We may feel ashamed or simply lack the energy to let others in. But we are missing out on one of the greatest blessings of the Christian life when we do that. So, let's get out there and connect, shall we?

APPLY IT: Do you have at least one or two people to share your faith walk with? If so, what can you do today to bolster those connections? If not, choose one step to take today: Join a small group at your church, ask a friend or acquaintance out for coffee, or ask God to bring you someone who will walk with you.

DAY
9

May your thoughts be as glad as the shamrocks.

May your heart be as light as a song.

May each day bring you bright happy hours,

That stay with you all year long.

—————— **TRADITIONAL IRISH BLESSING** ——————

TODAY'S READING: Proverbs 15:13, 15; Romans 15:13; Philippians 4:4–7

"Sure, I'd rather go to an Irish funeral over an Irish weddin' any day."

To say I was shocked by my friend's words would be an understatement. However, the sentiment is understandable. An Irish funeral is truly a celebration—complete with dancing, food, and laughter. Of course, there is heartache and grieving as well. But I can't help but feel the way the Irish approach funerals is the perfect example of the theme for today.

Sometimes I think Christians get happiness and joy confused. We feel that if we are sad, hurt, or grieving, we are falling short of God's call to live in joy. After all, joy is the second fruit of the Spirit (the evidence that will be clear in our life when we walk closely with God).

But the truth is, joy runs much deeper than simply a feeling. Happiness is dependent on our circumstances. Joy, on the other hand, stems from our identity in Christ and the deep, abiding understanding of all He's done for us. We have been rescued from sin, death, and hell and redeemed to a full, abundant, victorious life in Him now—and eternal life with Him when we die!

That, my friend, is true joy, unbothered by sadness, grief, stress, or pain. It is what allows us to stay rooted in our faith, no matter what we are experiencing. Even in the bleakest of hours, in the far depths of our soul, we can know we are safe, held, and loved.

At times, joy and happiness intersect and are evidenced on our faces, in the bubbling of our laughter, or in the flush of our cheeks as we celebrate or relish a long-awaited accomplishment.

Sometimes joy looks like dancing and shouting. Other times, it looks like holding the hand of a loved one as they pass from this world to the next while we sing hymns quietly at their bedside. It can look like curling up in the lap of our Father, alone in the dark, letting our tears soak His robes as we pour our heart out to Him.

Joy is our anchor. Joy is our compass. Joy is that first burst of air that fills our lungs as we break the surface of the flood after being pulled under. It is how we can live and walk out our faith victoriously, no matter the troubles that surround us. Oh, how I wish you that kind of joy, dear one. Today and always.

APPLY IT: Where is your joy meter today? Do you need to release the expectation of surface happiness and ask God to help you access the deeper joy planted in your soul? Take a moment to reflect on all that God has done for you, ask Him to make joy a can't-miss reality in your life, and thank Him in advance for it.

DAY
10

May you have warm words on a cold evening,

A full moon on a dark night,

And the road downhill all the way to your door.

TRADITIONAL IRISH BLESSING

TODAY'S READING: Psalm 18:30–36; Psalm 37:23–24; Psalm 119:105

I've never lived in an igloo, but I imagine the inside must be warmer than the first place we lived in Ireland. Built of cinder block with no insulation, that house radiated cold. Even though the windows were double-glazed and did a good job of blocking out the harsh natural elements so common to Donegal, the walls practically acted like an ice pack in a cooler. We used to close ourselves into the sitting room and get the fire roaring as high as possible. Then, right before bed, my husband would head to our bedroom, lift the covers, and spend a few minutes aiming the blow-dryer at them on full blast. He'd shout to me, and I'd sprint down the hall and jump under the covers right as he turned off the dryer and climbed in beside me. It was miserable. The one time our electricity went out during a winter storm made it even worse. We felt like we were freezing from the inside out. My bones were chilled, and it seemed like no matter what I did, nothing could warm up my core.

Has your soul ever felt that way? Like it's lost in the dark, shivering and miserable? No matter how many quiet times you have or sermons you sit through, nothing seems to "warm" up your soul? I've been there too. And that's the image that comes to mind when I read today's blessing.

The times in my life when I felt most adrift were amid periods of heavy transition or uncertainty. When the path for me or my family seemed shrouded in mist and darkness and I had no idea how to take the next step, let alone find the right path to follow. That's why I love today's Scriptures so much!

When I let the reality take root in my heart that God is my shield when I take refuge in Him (Ps. 18:30) and that He supports me with His hand, even and especially when I fall (Ps. 37:24), it's like a spark falling on a forest floor long devoid of rain. But I have to show up and make the choice to hide myself in Him.

I know it can feel foreign, even disingenuous, to sit with our Bibles and pray when our soul feels like doing anything but. However, spending time with the Father will shine that light on the path before us, and it is His Word that will warm our hearts on those dark nights of the soul. In my experience, feeling always follows faith. Meaning, when I am faithful to show up, read, pray, and talk to God—even when it feels like the last thing I want to be doing—the icy shield around my heart cracks and warmth begins to return.

So, if you're in a dark, frigid place right now, I encourage you to keep showing up, sweet friend. You're here already so just keep going. Eventually the warmth will return.

APPLY IT: If you are in that cold place today, choose one of today's verses and pray it back to God, asking Him to light your way and warm your soul. If you're not in that place, ask God to show you how to bring warmth and light to someone who is.

DAY
11.

Here's to a fellow who smiles
when life runs along like a song.
And here's to the lad who can smile
when everything goes dead wrong.

TRADITIONAL IRISH BLESSING

TODAY'S READING: Psalm 46; 2 Timothy 3:1–5; 1 Peter 4:12–19

The Irish are known worldwide for their jovial spirits and lilting accents and music. But a quick search of their history will reveal that the life of the Irish people has rarely been anything but harsh, traumatic, and full of injustice. And yet their joy prevails.

All too often, especially in American culture, we equate hardship with punishment. We tend to think that if life is difficult, challenging, or discouraging, we must be doing something wrong. But today's blessing—and more importantly, God Himself—tells us that is not always the case.

Yes, sometimes the hardships we endure are of our own making as a result of our sin or mistakes. Still other times, hardship is a result of the sins of others. But many times—I'd venture to say most of the time—we endure hardship simply because that is just how life goes. In fact, hard times can be an indicator that we are heading in the right direction.

Knowing that we can and should expect troubles and pain should help us embrace both when they come, seeing them not as punishments but opportunities.

We talked a few days ago about how an Irish funeral can actually be one of the most joyous and celebratory occasions one can attend, but this lesson of joy through hardships is one the vast majority of Irish people have learned day by day. Even while enduring famine, slavery, illness, and a life of extreme minimalism, the joy, laughter, storytelling, and music the Irish are famous for have thrived.

And these things should be even more prevalent for every follower of Jesus! For we know Who has won the ultimate victory and holds our eternal future in His hands! God didn't just defeat death and hell and then leave us to our own devices until we get to Heaven. No! He walks with us, carries us, and supports us every step of the way. What better reason to smile, laugh, and have hope in the face of hardship?

Friend, if you are in the trenches of pain and suffering today, let me take your hand and lovingly turn your attention upward, to your Father. Your circumstances may not change overnight, but the strength you have as He carries you and your burdens can.

APPLY IT: If you're in the trenches today, pray and thank God for walking through hard times with you. Then ask Him to open your eyes to the good and joyful things throughout the day. When He shows them to you, thank Him! If things are going well for you, thank God for that kindness! Then ask Him to show you who needs an encouraging word, look, or touch, and follow through!

DAY
12

May there always be work for your hands to do.

May your purse always hold a coin or two.

May the hand of a friend always be near you.

May God fill your heart with gladness to cheer you.

TRADITIONAL IRISH BLESSING

TODAY'S READING: Psalm 90:16–17; John 6:27; Philippians 2:14–16; Colossians 3:22–24

"What do ye call Bob the Builder durin' a recession?" my friend asked me.

My eyes drifted toward the ceiling as I tried to think of some clever play on words. When none came to me, I shook my head. "I don't know. What?"

Her brown eyes glistened as she tried to suppress her lilting laughter. "Bob."

When we moved back to Galway after four years back in America, the country was just coming out of a massive recession in which all building and construction had basically halted. For a nation built on the backs of blue-collar laborers, it was devastating. It was then I realized that we never heard any of our friends complain about having to go to work.

I often wondered if that was due to the joy of being able to work after the recession or if it was deeper than that. After enduring the Great Hunger (i.e., the Great Famine or Potato Famine), and a whole host of other hardships, perhaps appreciating good work sort of became hardwired into Irish DNA.

This led me to think of myself. Of course I'm grateful for my job. I've been grateful for every job I've had. But it's never too long before the honeymoon wears off and work becomes something I have to do rather than something I get to do.

That's why today's Scriptures are so important. They remind me of several things:

1. My job is a gift from the Lord. It is one of the main ways He keeps His promise to provide for me like He does the birds of the trees and flowers of the fields (see Ps. 90:17; Matt. 6:26–29).
2. My boss or supervisor is not really who I work for. I should approach everything I do, including my job, as a way to worship God.
3. Sometimes God's provision is more spiritual than physical.

No matter where you find yourself today—heading to a job you dread, a job you love, or in a pit of worry because you don't know if you will have a job—approach everything through the lens of worship. Trust that God's provision will always come . . . it just might not be in the form you were expecting (or even hoping for).

APPLY IT: What is your biggest need when it comes to your work? Pull that image into your mind with as much detail as you can. Then imagine yourself laying it at the feet of Jesus, Who is on His throne. Spend a few minutes focusing on how good and great He is and praise Him for it.

DAY
13

May the blessings of light be upon you,

Light without and light within.

The blessed sunlight shine on you

And warm your heart

Till it glows like a great peat fire.

And in all your comings and goings,

May you ever have a kindly greeting,

From them you meet on the road.

TRADITIONAL CELTIC BLESSING

TODAY'S READING: Mark 9:14–29; John 20:24–29; Hebrews 11:1–3; 1 Peter 1:3–16

The people in our small village out in the west of Ireland never bothered with listening to the weather forecast.

"Why bother?" they'd say. "Ye can tell the weather just by lookin' at the church. If ye can't see the church, it's rainin'. And if ye can see the church, it's gonna rain soon."

I found the joke hilarious, because there's such an element of truth to it. As I've mentioned, Ireland is so green for a reason. Many reasons, actually—225 of them. (That's the average number of days it rains there.)

On the odd day when the sun would shine bright and the air would fill with warm humidity, locals would flock to the beach and ice cream stands. Some would even joke, asking if they'd been bad and what that huge ball of fire in the sky was.

It's easy to forget the sun exists there, because it is so rarely seen clearly.

If I'm honest, I often feel that way about God. I sometimes lament, wishing that I had lived during Bible times when I could've literally seen Jesus face-to-face, heard His voice, and so on. But today's Scriptures (and many others) remind me that had that been so, I still would have no guarantee I'd feel any more connected to Him than I do today.

An intimate relationship with Jesus is less about physical proximity and more about the proximity of your heart. Do you see yourself in the desperate father we read about in Mark 9? So often I find myself crying out, "I believe!" only to turn around and ask for the strength to truly believe.

But dare I say that is all our heavenly Father really asks of us—to let our hearts be in such a posture of worship and adoration that we aren't afraid to ask for help when we recognize our faith slipping. I can't help but believe He'd much rather us continually reach out to Him than witness us let our pride deceive us into thinking everything is okay when it's not.

So when the doubts creep in and you begin to wonder if your prayers are even making it past the ceiling or if He's forgotten about you and turned His thoughts to someone "holier" or "more deserving," keep crying out. I promise, He's far closer than you realize.

APPLY IT: Spend a few minutes thinking back over the last couple weeks and look for ways God has shown up faithfully. It could be something big, like a physical healing, or something small, like an unexpected, kind word from a coworker. Thank God for His closeness, even when you can't see/feel it.

DAY
14

We cannot share a sorrow

If we haven't grieved a while.

Nor can we feel another's joy

Until we've learned to smile.

TRADITIONAL IRISH BLESSING

TODAY'S READING: Exodus 17:8–13; Romans 15:1–6; 2 Corinthians 1:3–7; 1 Thessalonians 5:8–11

When our kids were seven, five, and two, we had to head back to the States for a while. We had to pack up our house so it would be okay with us gone for a few months. Then our oldest got a severe stomach flu, among a few other bumps in the road.

Our next-door neighbor had an incredible garden with all sorts of wonderful fresh vegetables and flowers. One afternoon just a few days before we were due to leave, there was a knock at our door. That neighbor was standing there with a basket of treasures from her garden slung over her arm.

"I just thought ye might use these," she said. "Save ya from havin' to run to the shop." And just as suddenly as she'd appeared, she was gone—without even staying for the obligatory, ahem, customary cuppa tea!

A few minutes later, there was another knock. This time it was our across-the-street neighbor bearing a large pot of stew. "To save ye havin' to cook and dirty up the whole kitchen," she said.

I accepted her offering through tears of gratitude. I was so moved at their kindnesses. They knew we were leaving for six months (which ended up turning into forever, which is a whole other story in itself), but they didn't know our daughter was sick or just how stressed I was with everything on my plate. They just had an inkling we needed some help and took action.

Similar things happened when the family matron down the road passed away. Very few words were spoken. Very few were needed. People just showed up with food, drinks, tissues, and cakes.

You see, our neighbors didn't know what we were experiencing as we tried to get our young family ready to cross the ocean yet again. But they'd had family move away and they'd raised children themselves. They knew from their own experiences that what we were doing was really, really hard. Good, but hard. And they wanted to help, even in as small a way as bringing dinner and the ingredients for a farm-fresh salad.

And that is exactly what we are called to do for one another within the body of Christ, as well as for our neighbors in the world. Our sorrow, grief, and joy is never wasted so long as we use it to fuel our service to others.

And, dare I say, we also need to be willing to accept it when it comes our way. It feels wrong somehow, and yet we rob our brothers and sisters of the joy of serving when we refuse their help.

APPLY IT: Look for someone to extend a kind act to today. And if you're struggling, be open to letting someone else minister to your heart. Ask God to open your eyes to who needs it most.

DAY
15

Bless you with the first light of sun

Bless you when the long day is done

Bless you in your smiles and your tears

Bless you through each day of your years.

TRADITIONAL IRISH BLESSING

TODAY'S READING: 1 Chronicles 4:10; Psalms 84; Ephesians 3:14–21; 3 John 1:2–4

Blessings come in all shapes and sizes. Some are material; some, emotional; still others, spiritual. I'll never forget the time we received an abundance of all three.

We were living in a small village on the coast of County Galway. We'd visited the States when our son was about five months old and had considered holding a baby dedication at a family member's church while there. But the more we talked and prayed about it, the more we really sensed God leading us to do it when we got back to Ireland.

If you're not familiar, during a baby dedication the parents go before the church and make a public commitment to raise their child according to God's Word. It doesn't provide any sort of salvation for the baby, rather it represents a collective commitment between the parents and the church to work together to raise the child in "the way they should go" (Prov. 22:6 NIV).

We were nervous about this for many reasons:

- The village we were in was primarily Catholic and therefore conducted christenings instead of dedications.
- We didn't have a local church and weren't sure where we would hold the event.
- We wondered if doing this would further set us apart as "those weird Yanks."

But God kept nudging, so we started brainstorming and continued praying. As soon as we took the first step to plan the dedication, the blessings started pouring in. First, our good friend and café owner, the first non-family member to hold our son after he was born, insisted on closing down his café on a Sunday afternoon—his busiest day—so we could hold the event there. He also insisted on providing the cake—free of charge. Another friend offered us her son's christening outfit. What an honor! (I've never been so terrified of my baby ruining a set of clothes before. Ha!) On the day of the event, the place was packed with our closest friends, neighbors, and community members.

But the biggest blessing of all came at the end when the café reopened. A lady walked in and asked our friend, who was an atheist at the time, what was going on. I stood by and listened as he shared that my husband and I were making a commitment to raise our son to know Who Jesus is so that when he is old enough, he can decide if he wants to follow Him. Then he added that they were all there in support and were happy to help us in any way they could.

Over a decade later, that memory still moves me to tears. That friend eventually ended up attending Bible studies and growing closer to God—all because of the Lord's provision and our willingness to take an awkward step of obedience.

APPLY IT: Is God nudging you to do something today? Share it with a trusted friend and take one step toward obedience.

DAY
16

Now sweetly lies old Ireland

Emerald green beyond the foam,

Awakening sweet memories,

Calling the heart back home.

TRADITIONAL IRISH BLESSING

TODAY'S READING: 2 Corinthians 5:6–9; Philippians 3:20–21; Hebrews 13:14–16

I stood in the heart of the city, trains whirring past. Dogs barking. A hundred languages mingled in the chilled, pre-spring air. I was in the middle of a vibrant, metropolitan city, but my heart was a million miles away. It roamed far green fields, sat on rock walls, and watched the fog roll in from the ocean. It cozied elbow to elbow with friends in a pub with lilting music, pungent air, and a steaming cup of tea. I stood in Vienna, but my heart longed for Ireland—for home.

I stood on a hill, wind whipping my hair, sheep bleating in defiance of the rain that incessantly pelted their coats. I was in the middle of one of the most beautiful countries, but my heart was a million miles away. It was roasting in the summer heat, lying poolside, gazing up at a forever-blue sky. It was in the desert with cacti stretched tall in the orange-red-violet glow of a Sonoran sunset. It was in the living room with kin, drinking memories in deep. I was standing on a hill in Ireland, but my heart longed for Arizona—for home.

Now I'm sitting in a pew, surrounded by people with hands lifted, hearts swollen—perhaps broken—with music swirling and words of praise and honor lifting high. I'm sitting among people I love, worshiping the God I love, but my heart is a million miles away. It's bowed low on golden streets, too awed to lift my gaze. It's strolling, weightless and carefree for the first time, hand in hand with my Savior, the most beautiful One ever seen. I'm finally at rest, finally full—perfectly whole—without an ounce of doubt or pain, not wondering if I am good enough. I'm sitting in a sanctuary in a beautiful church, but my heart longs for Heaven—for home.

Do you ever feel homesick? Out of place? Like something isn't quite right? The longer I live, the more I realize that I truly do not have a home here on this earth. Home is so many different places, with so many different people. And the less at home I feel wherever I am now, the more keenly aware I am that I have a permanent home ready and waiting for me. This spurs me on to want more—to not settle for just getting by on this spinning rock we call Earth. It makes me want to love more deeply, laugh more heartily, work more diligently, and care more freely, because in the blink of an eye this home will be no more, and I will finally be face-to-face with the One for Whom I loved, laughed, worked, and cared. I will finally be home.

So when you feel the pangs of sadness, when home just doesn't feel like home anymore, when you just can't seem to find your place here and you feel alone, find your place in Him. He loves without demand and will provide this forever home to anyone who asks—anyone who dares to love Him in return. And you know what? It's amazing how knowing where home truly is gives purpose and drive and reason to this season spent in a foreign land.

APPLY IT: Where are you feeling unsettled today? Lift that up to your heavenly Father and ask Him to guide you through it and to help you grow until it's time for you to go home.

DAY
17.

May those who love us, love us.

And those that don't love us,

May God turn their hearts.

And if He doesn't turn their hearts,

May he turn their ankles.

So we'll know them by their limping.

TRADITIONAL IRISH BLESSING

TODAY'S READING: Psalm 37:1–6; Matthew 5:43–47; Luke 6:27–28; Romans 12:18–21

Our first landlady in Ireland was one of the most unique individuals I've ever met. She had a window to the world from her front room, where she spent her days gazing out over the community. She knew everyone in the village, and everyone in the village knew her.

We knew moving into a small, rural village in Ireland was going to have some challenges, but when we first arrived it seemed people were giving us a wide berth wherever we went. It took almost a year of us proving our normalcy before we were accepted in our adopted home. It turns out that when our flight from the States had been delayed because of mechanical issues, causing us to arrive at our rental house almost twelve hours late, she told the community it was because we'd brought guns on the plane. That's right. She told our village that we were gunrunners for the IRA. I'm dead serious. You can't make this stuff up. Well . . . she could.

As you can imagine, that news was a bit disturbing to those in a village bordering Northern Ireland, which had very close ties to The Troubles. And it was even more difficult for us to learn of this lie after two years living under this woman's roof!

The whole "so we'll know them by their limping" thing from today's blessing has always made me chuckle. Why would we need to know our enemies or those who don't hold us in too high a regard? Is it so we can avoid them? Exact revenge? Maybe.

However, after praying through it, I believe it might have two uses. One, to help us to be wise. Once we knew our landlady's proclivity for making up details she didn't know, we took care to be very clear and up-front with her, but we were also careful with what extremely sensitive information we gave her. When we know the people we can trust, we can be wise in the ways we interact with them. The second and most important use for knowing our enemies is so we can pray for them. God is very clear in His Word that we are to heap coals of kindness on the heads of our enemies, serve them, and pray for them (see Rom. 12:20). This is not so we can be doormats but so we can be used by God to draw our enemies nearer to Him, which is our true calling as followers of Christ.

APPLY IT: Is there someone in your life who is "limping"? Take a few minutes to pray for them today—not for them to change but for them to know, love, and follow God.

DAY
18

A good laugh and a long sleep

are the best cures in the doctor's book.

TRADITIONAL IRISH BLESSING

TODAY'S READING: 1 Kings 19:3–8; Psalm 4:6–8; Psalm 126; Proverbs 17:22; Matthew 11:28–30

Among their other attributes (and perhaps stereotypes), the Irish are known the world over for their humor and joyous outlook on life. We even talked back on day 9 about how most Irish people would choose to go to a funeral over a wedding because of the joy that's infused into grief.

But I really think they're onto something. The Irish have one of the most brutal, oppressive histories on the planet, and yet their joie de vivre endures. They see the value in a good laugh, as well as a good rest. Sundays, traditionally, have been just that in Ireland—a day of rest. With shops closed (or set to close much earlier), the day is spent worshiping at church, then resting with family and friends.

Of course, the modern world has invaded, so that is not so much true in the big cities anymore, but even in the hustle and bustle of a place like Dublin, the pace of life is much slower, with relationships and laughter taking precedent.

I think we can learn a lot from that—and from the examples set for us in God's Word.

As I write this, I'm in a season of exhaustion. No matter how much I sleep, I never feel rested. And I've felt the pull in my spirit to explore other avenues of rest beyond sleep. I'm looking for ways to refuel my creativity and my spirit. I'm seeking joy and laughter—it's such a release! And slowly . . . *very* slowly . . . I'm beginning to see change.

But just watching a silly movie won't restore our souls. Our pursuits of renewal must be coupled with time with Jesus. Look at Elijah. He was ready to die, and then God led him to take a long nap, eat a couple snacks, and then head to a cave alone to be with God (see 1 Kings 19:4–8)!

Jesus did the same thing when the weight of the cross threatened to crush Him—He turned to time alone with God.

With the state of this world, sometimes laughter and joy feel insensitive or out of place, but God tells us there can be both at once. In fact, I'm going to give you one more bonus verse today. Proverbs 14:13 reads, "Even in laughter a heart may be sad, and joy may end in grief" (CSB).

You see, friend, joy is not ignoring the problems of this world. It's recognizing the victory that God has already overcome those problems, and even when it all looks bleak, we can trust and rejoice.

APPLY IT: What do you need more of—rest or laughter? Make a plan to seek out one today, using the lens of worship and gratitude for all God has done for you.

DAY
19

May you have the hindsight to know where you've been,

the foresight to know where you are going,

and the insight to know when you have gone too far.

TRADITIONAL IRISH BLESSING

One November afternoon, we set out on a scenic drive with a group of American friends. We had spent the day exploring the village of Dingle down on the Ring of Kerry and were heading back to the small village of Doolin in County Clare. Granted, this was before the days of GPS on our phones. In fact, only one or two of us even had a cell phone. Instead, we had to print directions. However, the route we decided to take didn't show up on the map. It was one the driver had heard about and thought would be cool to try.

Never mind that it was November, which meant the sun would set by 4:00 p.m. and the world would be pitch-black as we wound through seemingly endless hills and valleys. At first, we were excited, ready to enjoy a new corner of our beloved Emerald Isle. But as the roads grew narrower, and the sky grew darker, our spirit of adventure faded while what should've been a two-hour jaunt turned into five . . . maybe six.

We knew where we had been and we knew where we were trying to go. We were just lacking the insight to know when the new plan wasn't working before it was too late. So, not only was our route not scenic (because of the darkness), many of us ended up carsick, and we were all grumpy and exhausted by the time we returned. I'll give you three guesses what we remember most about that trip. (Hint: It's not the Guinness stew and handmade ice cream we had in Dingle.)

Does your life ever feel like that? You know exactly where you're headed, then either by your own choice or due to someone else's choices you find yourself in the middle of nowhere, with no end or destination in sight. And by the time you get to where you originally wanted to be, you can't even enjoy it?

I'll be honest, sometimes my faith journey has felt like that. But the good news is it doesn't have to continue. If you stay tethered to the One who created the map (and the road), the unexpected bumps on the journey of life will feel less like a life-threatening detour and more like an exciting adventure.

So, what do you do when you wake up one day and realize you're on an old, abandoned path in treacherous country you were never meant to be in?

1. Stop and admit to God that you've lost your way.
2. Ask Him to open your eyes to the right path and to guide you to it.
3. Stay tethered to the Cartographer, spending time daily in His Word and in conversation with Him.

APPLY IT: Are you feeling lost today, friend? Work through the three steps above and spend time sharing your heart with God. Then choose one of today's Scriptures and make it your prayer for the day, week, or even the rest of the month.

DAY
20

May the Lord keep you in His hand

and never close His fist too tight.

TRADITIONAL IRISH BLESSING

TODAY'S READING: Psalm 139; Isaiah 41:10, 13; John 10:27–29

Every place we lived in Ireland, we could see the ocean from our living room window. But it was our first house, out in the wilds of Donegal, that often comes to mind when I think of our time there. For a desert girl raised in the arid Arizona climate, the sheer power of wild weather in Donegal was awe-inspiring. And terrifying.

I remember gazing out the double-glazed windows and watching the sea change with the weather's fickle moods. When the winds were really strong, our car would rock and shake in the driveway out front, and I would often fear it was going to get swept away like a deleted scene from *The Wizard of Oz*. And at night, the whole house seemed to shake like thunder from the incredible strength of the wind. Then the dreams started.

The location changed from dream to dream. Sometimes I was in a house of glass; other times, I stood on a rock jetty right on the shore, watching helplessly as a tsunami built on the horizon and hurtled my way. When I was on the jetty,

I'd brace as the wave crashed over me, only to find myself still standing there. Then it would build and crash again. And so the dream would go, over and over, until I awoke. In the dreams when I was in the glass house, the gales drove massive wave after massive wave crashing against the fragile structure, and I just knew at any minute the walls would shatter and I'd be overtaken. But they never did. I never was.

I remember talking to a pastor friend about these dreams, because I was having them almost nightly—which, as you can imagine, was exhausting. My friend didn't have any sort of holy, Daniel-like interpretation for me, but he did think that deep down, I was overwhelmed emotionally and spiritually. But the fact that I was never swept away or destroyed by the storms indicated that I also knew I was ultimately safe in God's hands.

I don't have those dreams anymore, but many times since then, when I have felt overwhelmed and stuck in a storm I couldn't escape, I've been reminded of their message: God holds me fast in His mighty right hand. If you are a follower of Jesus, my dear friend, that same hand holds you too. No matter the storm surging around you today, remember that you are held fast. And there's no safer place for your spirit to reside. We just have to remember that our ultimate good often looks different than we'd expect (or perhaps even want).

APPLY IT: Are you facing a storm today, friend? Stand before your Father and declare your trust in Him to hold you through it, even when it seems hopeless. If you cannot fully declare that trust, be honest and share that you want to trust Him, then ask Him to help you. If you don't have the words, borrow them from today's Scriptures and pray them back to God.

DAY
21

May the hand of a friend always be near you.

And may God fill your heart with gladness to cheer you.

TRADITIONAL IRISH BLESSING

TODAY'S READING: Ecclesiastes 4:9–12; Matthew 18:19–20; Hebrews 10:24–25

One of the hardest things about our time in Ireland was the lack of places to worship. The only house of worship available to us way out in the rural villages where we lived was not the same denomination we normally subscribe to.

We didn't attend often, but on a few Easters, Christmases, and the odd regular Sunday morning, we would go there—and it was always such a blessing. Despite being of a different tradition, and in a different language (Irish Gaelic), it was so wonderful to gather with others with the sole purpose of worshiping God.

Other times, we gathered in homes with the few people who shared our faith and prayed, read Scripture, and broke bread together. But outside of Sundays, we were surrounded by people who loved God and often spoke blessings and prayers over one another. Nevertheless, I can't tell you how many times I prayed with those professing to be atheists. Those moments were truly beautiful.

I think such things are so welcome by most because we were designed to be in community. We were never meant to live as an island or a hermit, only "connecting" with others through a screen.

Don't get me wrong. I'm grateful for modern technology and how it allows me to stay in contact with people I love all around the world. But that should not, and cannot, be my only means of community.

After the pandemic, my family struggled to get back into the routine and habit of attending church in person. It was so nice to just roll out of bed, snuggle on the couch, and watch church in our jammies. Even for me, a mega-extrovert, it was just so . . . comfortable. Getting up and out the door just felt too hard. Like too much work. But you know what, once we forced ourselves back out of our comfort zone and actually darkened the door of the church, our relationships blossomed. The sense of dread and loneliness that had settled over my heart began to dissipate.

Friend, even the most introverted among us was created with an innate need for community. Yes, it can be a lot of work. And it can be tiring at times, but when challenges and struggles come, it is so sweet to be able to rely on my brothers and sisters in Christ to help carry me through. And, likewise, to be able to rally around someone else in need, or in celebration, is such a sweet, sacred thing.

APPLY IT: Do you have any like-minded loved ones near at hand? What can you do to deepen those relationships? If you've gotten out of the habit of gathering with others, I encourage you to reach out today. Send a text of encouragement or reconnection and make a plan to gather with other believers this week.

DAY
22

May God surround you with all that is good

And may you share it with as many as you could.

TRADITIONAL IRISH BLESSING

TODAY'S READING: Luke 21:1–4; 2 Corinthians 9:10–15;
1 Timothy 6:17–19; 1 Peter 4:7–11

I've already shared how generous our Irish neighbors were
with us, bringing us bounty from their gardens, food from
their kitchens, and more. And it just seems that generosity
was built into every member of that community by nature.

The first time I met the woman who would become my
best friend there, she invited us to her house for dinner.
This was no small feat, as she had five children of her own
who ranged in age from two to early teens. So arriving to
a home-cooked feast of pot roast, more types of potatoes
than we could count, veg, and dessert was such a generous
blessing!

And everyone we met was like that. God blessed us
with such a wonderful community of people who could
call on one another when work ran long and they needed
someone to pick up the baby from daycare or to drop
over some spuds when we ran out and had people on
the way over. It reminded me of that time in Acts 2 when
the church members sold all their belongings and shared

everything they had with one another. It seemed like that was the mindset of our Irish community.

What does that look like for us today? Is God saying we need to sell all our stuff and go live in a commune somewhere? Perhaps. Maybe for some of us. But for most of us, I think it looks like living life with an open hand, being ready to give to others as God leads.

If our fists are clenched tightly around our money, resources, belongings, time, and talents, when God wants to provide for someone through us, there's a good chance we will miss the opportunity.

I remember one time, I'd walked down the street to get food from one of my favorite takeaway places. I'd been thinking about it all day, and I couldn't wait to sink my teeth into the delicious ambrosia that awaited me. But as I walked home, I passed a homeless man, and I felt a nudge in my spirit to give my food to him. I'm ashamed to say, I paused. After all, I'd been looking forward to that meal all day. And we weren't in a place financially that I could just go back and get more. But the Lord kept nudging, so I obeyed. I never saw that man again, and I have no idea what ramifications that meal had for him. All I know is that God clearly told me to give.

Giving isn't just about money or possessions. Often we are commanded to give our time, energy, and companionship—

which can be more difficult to part with than our money! But it's always so much better to give when prompted, as your spirit will be blessed just as much as the person receiving. Obedience always deepens our relationship with our Father.

APPLY IT: Take a few minutes and list some of the ways God has been generous with you. It could be materially, spiritually, financially, etc. Thank Him for these gifts and ask Him to show you where and how He wants you to be generous today. And when He leads, act.

DAY
23

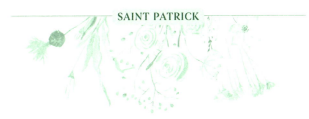

May the strength of God pilot us,
may the wisdom of God instruct us,
may the hand of God protect us,
may the word of God direct us.
Be always ours this day and forevermore.

SAINT PATRICK

TODAY'S READING: Job 12:7–10; Psalm 32:8; 73:26–28; John 14:1–6

Red sails glide effortlessly along the water of the bay, criss-crossing and zigzagging their way to and from the ocean. Even in the roughest weather, these boats sail, seemingly unfazed by the turmoil around them. On the blusteriest days, I often wondered if I'd find Jesus sleeping peacefully in the bottom of one of the Hooker boats that famously call Galway home.

"How can they sail in this?" I asked a friend one day.

"Easy," he replied. "They were built for it."

You see, the Galway Hooker boats (named for the "hook and line" fishing method used by the men who sailed them) were specifically designed to withstand the perils of Irish waters. In fact, in 1954 the *Connaught Tribune* newspaper said, "To those who know the strength of the sea and its un-relenting cruelty [the Hooker boat] has always meant safety. Because they were good boats and blessed with good luck." *

---

*As quoted in "The Galway Hooker," Galway City Museum, accessed March 25, 2025, https://galwaycitymuseum.ie/exhibition/the-galway-hooker/.

And the same can be said of you, dear friend. You were designed with purpose, for a purpose. God knew you would be exactly where you are now, and He equipped you with everything you need to fulfill His calling on your life. If you allow His strength to guide you, His wisdom and Word to instruct and direct you, and His hand to protect you, you will not succumb to the wind and waves this world hurls at you.

You were not only designed with purpose—you are unique! To the untrained eye, all the red and black sails of the Hooker boats look the same, but there are, indeed, four different types of Hookers, each used for a specific purpose. And so it is with you. God designed you with a unique purpose and plan that only you can fulfill. You bring specific gifts and talents to your family, your job, your community, and the body of Christ.

So, while it might feel like the waves are going to crash over and pull you under, you were designed to withstand the obstacles in your path, as you rely on His strength and guidance.

APPLY IT: Which aspect of God's character resonates with you most: His strength, His wisdom, His protection, or His Word? Take a moment to reflect on how you've seen that attribute at work in your life and thank Him for it. Then spend a few minutes in prayer, preparing your heart for any obstacles that will come your way today.

DAY
24

For each petal on the shamrock,

This brings a wish your way.

Good health, good luck, and happiness

For today and every day.

TRADITIONAL IRISH BLESSING

TODAY'S READING: 1 Corinthians 13:13; Hebrews 6:13–20; Hebrews 11:1 (actually, just read the whole chapter ☺); 1 John 4:15–16

One of my favorite stories from the life of Saint Patrick is how he used the shamrock to explain the Trinity. People often struggle to wrap their minds around the Trinity. How can there be three separate entities but still just one God? Wiser ones than I have worked for years to answer that question, so I won't venture to do so here.

But I chose today's Irish blessing because it conjures similar images in my mind to that of Saint Patrick's object lesson.

It's no secret that the Irish are well known for their reliance upon luck—or lack thereof. Much of that is a stereotype, but I'd say there is a thread of truth behind it. So I want to take a moment today to look at this blessing more closely.

What if we tweak it just a bit? Instead of a wish, what if we think of it as a prayer? And what if we replace health and luck and happiness (which can all be fleeting in even the most devout and faithful followers of God) with the three things God says will remain: faith, hope, and love (1 Cor. 13:13).

And just as Saint Patrick encouraged us to look at the three leaves of the shamrock and see the triune God, I encourage you to look and see how each member of the Godhead connects to these three that remain.

Hebrews 11:1 tells us that *faith* "is the reality of what is hoped for, the proof of what is not seen" (CSB). The rest of the chapter goes on to outline how heroes of the faith proved that reality from verse 1 over and over again. And it was by the strength of the Holy Spirit that they were able to do so.

Before that, Hebrews 6 talks about the *hope* that Abraham had because of the promises God made to him, and then how we can and do have that same hope because of the things God has promised us and secured through Jesus. Not only does the hope of His fulfilled promises encourage us, but they're an anchor for us. The hope holds us steady in unsteady times.

And then comes *love*. Today's verse from 1 Corinthians tell us that the greatest of the three that remain is love. And 1 John 4:16 spells it out for us: God is love. As my dad says, as H_2O is to water, so God is to love. Our heavenly

Father is literally made up of love. Oh, what a sweet realization, is it not, friend?

So, whenever you see a shamrock, remember the Trinity, and remember the great hope you can have because of your faith in God's promises, secured in His love.

APPLY IT: Which aspect of God's character do you need to sit with today? Take some time to revel in His presence and His promises.

DAY
25

May you see God's light on the path ahead

When the road you walk is dark.

May you always hear,

Even in your hour of sorrow,

The gentle singing of the lark.

When times are hard may hardness

Never turn your heart to stone,

May you always remember

When the shadows fall—

You do not walk alone.

TRADITIONAL IRISH BLESSING

TODAY'S READING: Matthew 17:14–20; Romans 10:17; Hebrews 10:32–39; 11:6; 1 John 5:1–4

When we had to leave Ireland unexpectedly, we found ourselves in a no-man's-land of sorts. We weren't sure if we would be able to return, and the stress of that uncertainty took a toll on our family. But it wasn't until we knew for sure that we wouldn't be going back that my faith really took a hit.

We had moved to Ireland because we sensed God was asking us to. To this day, I don't doubt that call. However, I also believed we would be there for the rest of our lives—or at least until we retired. So the abrupt end to that life threw me into a crisis of faith.

I was constantly second-guessing God and myself. Did I really hear Him right when He called us to the Emerald Isle? Suddenly I felt like I could really relate to Adam and Eve in a new way as whispers from every direction hissed, "Did God really say _____?"

Then came the anger. "God, you said _____!"

"God, why?"

"Did we do something wrong?"

We are more than a decade removed from that painful time, and only now can I see small shreds of why things went down the way they did. We lost money, we lost our home, and we lost precious time. We felt like we lost touch with friends as our community in Ireland doesn't use social media. Overnight, our community and lifeline were severed from us.

But looking back, I can unequivocally say the loss of my faith was the hardest blow. I didn't stop believing in God, nor did I renounce Jesus. But I questioned every last thing. And it was exhausting.

I think that's why Hebrews 11:6 says that it's impossible to please Him if we don't have faith. Because how can we obey if we are questioning and second-guessing everything He says and does? How can we be salt and light to those around us when we are wallowing in the depths of selfish navel-gazing?

Now, don't hear me say that hardship is always because of something we did or didn't do. God brings us through the occasional dark night of the soul. And doubts and questions are not wrong in and of themselves. But it's when we get into a pattern of doubt and despair that we lose the light and joy He brings. And, conversely, it's when we lean into trusting Him that His light and joy can return to our hearts.

APPLY IT: Are you struggling today, friend? Is your faith hanging on by a thread? Bring it to Him and allow Him to fortify your faith where you can't. Spend some time reflecting on the ways you've seen Him move in your life. Go back to the last thing He said to you. Ruminate on what you know to be true and ask Him to strengthen your faith like only He can.

DAY
26

May the dreams you hold dearest

be those which come true;

the kindness you spread,

keep returning to you.

TRADITIONAL IRISH BLESSING

TODAY'S READING: Psalm 37:1–6; Proverbs 16:1–4; Ephesians 2:1–10; Philippians 1:6, 9–11

It was never a dream of mine to live in Ireland. In fact, when I had to choose a foreign language to take in high school, I chose Spanish even though I really wanted to learn French.

What good is it to learn French when I'm never going to live where they speak it? I asked myself. *I live in southern Arizona. Spanish is the much more logical choice.*

Funny thing about God—He's rarely logical. A God of order, yes. Faithful, undoubtedly. Predictable . . . not so much.

Fast-forward fifteen years and I was standing at an airport on mainland Europe, wishing I'd taken those French classes after all.

You've heard about how to make God laugh, right? Make a plan. I feel like my whole life is a reflection of that sentiment. Very little has gone how I presumed it would. And I thank God for it! I never dreamed I'd live in Ireland, but that's where He led us. And it was during that time that He planted the seed of a dream to write in my heart. It would be another fifteen years before that dream came to fruition, but I don't believe He would have given me that desire had we not experienced what we did our first two years overseas.

That's the thing about this faith journey. Our wants, desires, and dreams shift and change as we grow and mature in our faith.

Sometimes we try to use Psalm 37 to manipulate God into giving us what we want. The thing is, the more we get to know Him so we can delight in Him, the more our wants and dreams will line up with His.

That can be scary to think about sometimes, can't it? If there's something you've dreamed of for years, it can be a bit terrifying to be willing to hold that dream with an open hand and let God mold, shape, tweak, or remove it as He aligns our heart with His. After all, what if that dream isn't part of His plan?

Here's the beauty: When we truly let our heart grow as He leads, we really will begin to want the same things He does. And if that dream is in line with His plans, wonderful. And if it is not, when we are rooted in Him and growing closer to Him, we will begin to see His plans unfold and that idea will become less desirable to us.

APPLY IT: Have you been carrying a dream that you have yet to see come to fruition? Place it at God's feet today and ask Him to help you trust in His timing and plan, then truly delight in Him and His ways.

DAY
27

Deep peace of the running wave to you.

Deep peace of the flowing air to you.

Deep peace of the quiet earth to you.

Deep peace of the shining stars to you.

Deep peace of the gentle night to you.

Moon and stars pour their healing light on you.

Deep peace of Christ,

of Christ the light of the world to you.

Deep peace of Christ to you.

TRADITIONAL IRISH BLESSING

TODAY'S READING: Psalm 19; Psalm 33:1–9; John 14: 27–31; 2 Thessalonians 3:16

As I mentioned on day 2, I used to be a runner. Some might say once a runner, always a runner, but that's not the case for me. Running in Ireland felt like running in Heaven . . . except, well, I hope we won't have to run in Heaven unless it's to see Jesus.

But there was just something about running in Ireland— the ocean waves, the misty air kissing my cheeks, the quiet fields surrounding me like a blanket—that brought me an overwhelming sense of peace. Some of my most intimate times of worship took place on those outings.

Once we returned to the States, I tried to get back into running, but I just couldn't. There was something about running along the streets of Phoenix that I found a far cry less inspiring than the hills and shores of the Emerald Isle. I can't imagine what it was. #Sarcasm

I think that's why today's blessing resonates so deeply with me. Even as a hardcore indoor girl, I have to admit there is just something about being in God's creation that sinks the reality of His presence and His goodness deeper into my soul like nothing else can.

Of course, we must be careful that we worship the Creator and not His creation, but when we truly open our eyes, His fingerprints are so clear and obvious that worshiping Him isn't an issue.

Take a moment to reread today's blessing. Go ahead, I'll wait.

Did you just take a deep, cleansing breath? I did—and peace washed over me.

We certainly need more peace, don't we? So how do we find it? The answer is right there, in the blessing, and in God's Word. Peace is found in Him. That's why I believe the author of this blessing repeats "Deep peace of Christ to you." It is in and through Him that true peace abides and abounds.

APPLY IT: Choose one of today's Scriptures and pray it over the area of your life or your heart that most needs His peace.

DAY
28

May the saddest day of your future

be no worse than the happiest day of your past.

TRADITIONAL IRISH BLESSING

TODAY'S READING: 1 Corinthians 13:9–12; 2 Corinthians 4:17–18; 1 John 3:1–3

If you're a follower of Jesus, this blessing is one hundred percent true for you—eternally speaking, that is!

When God promises in Romans 8:28 that all things work together for the good of those who love Him, He means it! And the good of which He speaks is our ultimate and eternal good.

So, if you've confessed that Jesus is Lord and believe God raised Him from the dead, what lies ahead of you is far, far greater than what is behind.

When we realized we would not return to Ireland, I went through one of the hardest, darkest periods of my life. It was like grieving the death of a loved one. We had completely invested our lives in that land and in her people, and we fully expected to live alongside them. I don't wish the grief that swelled in the years that followed on anyone, not even my worst enemy.

But what we will experience at the end of this life if we don't follow Jesus is infinitely worse than any grief or pain we could ever experience here. And I don't say that to scare you; I say it because I care for you.

If you've never put your faith wholly in Jesus, turn to page 149 and read more about how you can do that.

If you have given your life to Christ, then what was once a scary, heavy thought now frees and uplifts. Because we know that, in and through Christ, what awaits us in Heaven makes the troubles of the earth pale and fade.

As we've talked about before, that does not mean that our struggles and trials in this life aren't real or are insignificant. But remembering what awaits us when we will finally see God face-to-face and spend eternity in His true presence helps us carry the burdens of this life. We begin to understand what Paul meant when he said that the troubles and hardship of this life start to seem more like light and momentary afflictions when compared to the glory ahead of us (see 2 Cor. 4:17–18).

Breathe deep, my friend, and let that reality wash over you. I pray that it lightens you, as it is doing for me even as I write this. Whatever burdens you may be carrying— and many of us carry weighty burdens and griefs—Jesus knows, sweet one. He cares, and He will carry them until the weight of this world is no more.

APPLY IT: Spend a few moments today letting the reality of your eternity sink in. If you've given your life to Christ, let the joy and awe wash over you anew, and thank Him for His sacrifice that makes it possible. If you've not done that, turn to page 149 and read how you can.

DAY
29

May the blessing of light be on you—

light without and light within.

May the blessed sunlight shine on you

and warm your heart

till it glows like a great peat fire.

TRADITIONAL IRISH BLESSING

TODAY'S READING: Psalm 18:28; Matthew 5:14–16; John 1:1–5; 8:12; 1 Peter 2:9

We lived in a rural area of Ireland that is clothed in unspeakable beauty. Mountains, lakes, rivers, the ocean, bogland—it all merges together to create a landscape like none other. The homes and business there are built around the land, rather than carving through it. Homes can often be more than one hundred yards apart. It can be freeing. And it can be paralyzing.

In the dark bleakness of winter, it sometimes felt like a life sentence of solitary confinement.

Then it happened.

Driving home in the smothering darkness one night, a blue twinkle in the distance caught my eye. A moment later red, yellow, and orange danced brilliantly in the night. A quick scan of the horizon revealed half a dozen such displays. Christmas lights. More than that—signs of life. It was as if I had finally reached the surface of the water and emerged, gasping. My lungs finally able to fill with air. A release. I wasn't alone.

Never before had so simple a thing as a strand of Christmas lights brought such relief to my spirit. And it brought to mind Matthew 5:16. For some reason I've always thought of the instructions in that verse as something sort of passive. If Christ is in your heart, as long as you don't intentionally try to cover Him up or hide Him, His light will shine and others will know there's something different about you.

Now, however, I read that verse differently. The only reason the drive home that night became less lonely is because someone had taken the effort to turn on the lights.

How many other people, Jesus followers or not, are driving down the proverbial road, paralyzed by the weight of darkness surrounding them? How many feel utterly alone, surrounded by throngs of people and yet shrouded in the abyss of loneliness? If I—someone who has the miraculous Light of the World abiding within my very being—can feel the weight of loneliness, how much more paralyzed might someone be who doesn't know of His freeing power?

We must offer hope. We must actively reach out in support, encouragement, and service to those who have been placed in our path. It's not enough to have the light of Christ—we must hang it up, turn it on, and offer it freely, abundantly, and actively to those standing with us in the abyss.

APPLY IT: Take a few moments and thank God for the gift of the Light of the World, then ask Him to show you how you can be a light of encouragement to someone today. And if you're feeling stuck in the abyss, ask Him to help you see His light.

DAY
30

May the hand of God protect me,

the way of God lie before me,

the shield of God defend me,

the host of God save me.

May Christ shield me today.

SAINT PATRICK

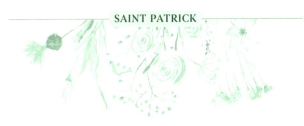

TODAY'S READING: Romans 5:1–5; Colossians 3:12–17; 1 John 4:7–18

Oh, dear friend, can you believe we are already nearing the end of our time together? It has been the highest honor for me to spend this time with you. And this blessing seemed fitting for our penultimate day together.

It reminds me of something Saint Patrick said, according to the Confession of Saint Patrick: "[God] watched over me before I knew him, and before I learned sense or even distinguished between good and evil, and he protected me, and consoled me as a father would his son."*

If you don't know Saint Patrick's story, here's a brief summary. He was born in Wales, not Ireland. But he was kidnapped by Vikings and taken to Ireland to work as a slave. At one point, Patrick escaped and returned to Wales, where he began studying to be a priest. But one night he dreamed that his former captors were begging him to return and share the gospel with them. So he did!

---

*Saint Patrick, "Confession of St. Patrick," accessed January 2, 2025, https://www.ccel.org/ccel/patrick/confession.ii.html.

Can you imagine the faith, trust, and . . . well, guts that had to take? And what a gift it was for Patrick to recognize that God had been watching over him—even before he believed in God—and orchestrating things so that he could share the gospel with a whole nation!

That type of experience isn't just for saints of old either. If God led you to pick up this devotional, He was calling you to Himself. Not because my words carry any special powers—on the contrary! My only goal is to point you back to the God Who loves you.

But if you've yet to decide to follow Christ, I pray that your heart is moved by the reality that He is calling you, seeking you. He wants to bring you into a right relationship with Him.

If you are already a follower of Christ, I pray that this reminder bolsters your faith and reminds you that He loves you more than any other. And He longs to abide in and with you.

Because, as we've seen these last thirty days, it is only by remaining in Christ, and through the power of His Spirit, that we can do anything.

I pray that today's blessing will be deeply true in your life as you seek to remain in Jesus like a branch clings to a vine, and as you share His love with your family, your friends, and your community.

APPLY IT: How can you abide in God today? How can you let His love abide in you? Choose one of today's Scriptures and write it out as a prayer back to Him.

DAY
31

Christ with me,
Christ before me,
Christ behind me,
Christ in me,
Christ beneath me,
Christ above me,
Christ on my right,
Christ on my left,
Christ when I lie down,
Christ when I sit down,
Christ when I arise,
Christ in the heart of every man who thinks of me,
Christ in the mouth of everyone who speaks of me,
Christ in every eye that sees me,
Christ in every ear that hears me.

SAINT PATRICK

TODAY'S READING: Acts 17:24–28; 1 Corinthians 8:6; Colossians 1:15–20

It is no accident that today's blessing falls on the final day of this devotional. On the contrary, that choice was very intentional, because the whole point of this devotional is to point you to Jesus and for you to hopefully draw closer to Him through His Word and through our time together.

As we've talked about at length already, we truly cannot do anything in this life apart from Christ; He is why and how we live and move and have our being. He is love. He is the source of our faith. He is our anchor of hope. And I pray you know Him better today than you did when you started this journey.

Take a moment to review today's blessing. I encourage you to read it out loud, gesturing with each direction mentioned. Then close your eyes and envision what these words actually mean. What does it look like to be fully surrounded and encompassed by Jesus?

Now, take a look back at Colossians 1:17: "[Jesus] is before all things, and by him all things hold together" (CSB).

I love how the Message says it: "He was there before any of it came into existence and holds it all together right up to this moment."

In the previous verse, God tells us that "all things have been created through him and for him" (CSB).

All things—that means you, dear one. God not only created you, He is also holding you together, even right now. Anyone feel like they're one small crisis away from completely falling apart? Yeah, me too.

The good news is He won't let you! He's surrounding you, lifting you up, and holding you together.

APPLY IT: For the remainder of our time together, I invite you to sit in His presence and reflect on these truths, as well as all He has shown you this month.

GET TO KNOW JESUS

Oh, friend, I am so grateful you're here! If you have never placed your faith in Jesus, I'd love to walk you through what that means and how to do it. As you prepare to read these next passages, I pray that God will open the eyes of your heart to see His goodness and grace.

When God created the world, the first people (Adam and Eve) made a choice that changed the course of humanity forever. They chose to disobey God's orders (see Gen. 3).

From that moment on, sin—anything that goes against the will of God—had entered the bloodline of humanity. I know sin is a big, dirty-sounding church word these days, but it just means to "miss the mark" and comes from a Greek word that could be used in the context of archery.*

*Strong's Lexicon, "hamartia," https://www.blueletterbible.org/lexicon/g266/kjv/tr/0-1/.

And God says every single person has missed the mark of His best. We see this in Romans 3:23, which says: "For all have sinned and fall short of the glory of God."

We have all done things we shouldn't have and not done things we should have. I certainly have! Think of the best person you know. The one who makes you think, *Oh, yeah, they're a really good person. They're for sure going to Heaven.* Well, I have news for you. That person has sinned, too.

And that sin keeps us separated from God. But He created us. We are His children, and He wants a relationship with us. So He sent His son Jesus to pay the price for our sins. Jesus lived a perfect, sinless life (the only person ever to do so!) and then He died a horrible death on the cross to pay the penalty for what we've done wrong.

Romans 6:23 tells us, "The wages of sin is death, but the gift of God is eternal life in Christ Jesus our Lord" (CSB). And in Romans 5:8 we get the best news: "while we were still sinners, Christ died for us."

This is exactly what we were talking about on day 30! You don't have to clean yourself up before you come to Him! He died for you (and for me) while you were still sinning and hurting Him!

So, what do we do now?

Romans 10:9 promises that "if you confess with your mouth that Jesus is Lord and believe in your heart that God raised him from the dead, you will be saved."

Because Jesus already paid the price for our mistakes and shortcomings, there's nothing else we can do to earn His love—we already have it! All we have to do is believe that He is Who He says He is and confess that we have sinned. This gift is available to anyone who will believe.

When we do that, "we have peace with God through our Lord Jesus Christ" (Rom. 5:1).

Will you believe today, my dear friend? If so, tell Him! Confess to Jesus that you believe He is the only Son of God, that He died to pay the price for your sins, and that you accept the forgiveness He purchased for you on the cross. Tell Him you want to follow Him and let Him be the boss of your life.

If you did this today, please drop me a line and let me know at Jennifer@JenniferDeibel.com. I'd love to celebrate with you!

If you'd like to continue learning about what God has to say about following Christ, you can read more here:

- *What is sin?* Romans 3:10–18
- *How can I be sure I've been forgiven?* Romans 8:1, 38–39; 10:13

- *How do I follow Jesus?* Luke 9:23–24; John 8:31–38; 13:34–35; 1 John 2:3–6
- *How do I pray (talk to God)?* Philippians 4:6–7; Hebrews 4:16; 1 John 5:14
- *Should I attend church?* Matthew 18:20; Colossians 3:12–17; Hebrews 10:19–25

JENNIFER DEIBEL is the award-winning author of *A Dance in Donegal, The Lady of Galway Manor, The Maid of Ballymacool, The Irish Matchmaker,* and *Heart of the Glen.* With firsthand immersive experience abroad, Jennifer writes stories that help redefine home through the lens of culture, history, and family. After nearly a decade of living in Ireland and Austria, she now lives in Arizona with her husband and their three children.

Connect with Jen:

JenniferDeibel.com   @JenniferDeibelAuthor

@JenniferDeibel_Author

BOOKS BY JENNIFER DEIBEL

A Dance in Donegal

The Lady of Galway Manor

The Maid of Ballymacool

The Irish Matchmaker

Heart of the Glen

NONFICTION

May the Road Rise to Meet You:
A 31-Day Devotional Inspired by Irish Blessings